SOFTBALL

Softball: Rules of the Game

Barbara Bonney

The Rourke Corporation, Inc.
Vero Beach, Florida 32964

© 1998 The Rourke Corporation, Inc.

All rights reserved. No part of this book may be reproduced or utilized in any form or by any means, electronic or mechanical including photocopying, recording or by any information storage and retrieval system without permission in writing from the publisher.

Barbara Bonney is a librarian and freelance writer in Cincinnati, Ohio. Besides enjoying research and words, she likes creating with food and fabrics. She has two children.

PHOTO CREDITS:
© Tony Gray: cover, pages 6, 7, 12, 13, 15, 16, 19, 22; © East Coast Studios: pages 4, 9, 10, 18, 21

EDITORIAL SERVICES:
Susan Albury

Library of Congress Cataloging-in-Publication Data

Bonney, Barbara, 1955-
   Softball—rules of the game/ by Barbara Bonney.
     p. cm. — (Softball)
   Includes index
   Summary: Outlines the main rules in the game of softball.
   ISBN 0-86593-481-9
   1. Softball—Rules—Juvenile literature. [1. Softball—Rules. 2. Softball.]
I. Title. II. Series: Bonney, Barbara, 1955- Softball.
GV881.2.B66 1998
796.357'8—dc21   98–11086
                                                                                      CIP
                                                                                       AC

Printed in the USA

TABLE OF CONTENTS

Softball vs. Baseball 5

The Field and Equipment 6

Players and Substitutes 8

The Game 11

Pitching 12

Batting 14

Base Running 17

Umpires 18

Dead Ball, Alive Ball 20

Glossary 23

Index 24

SOFTBALL VS. BASEBALL

Softball is similar to baseball. They are both played on a diamond-shaped field, the ball is hit with a bat, and players run around the bases to score before getting called out. Softball diamonds are smaller than baseball diamonds, and there is no pitcher's mound, just a pitching plate on flat ground. Some of the equipment is different too. A softball game lasts just seven **innings** (IN ingz) compared to nine in baseball.

Softball must be pitched underhand but that doesn't always slow the ball. In fast-pitch softball, pitches can be faster than in baseball.

The team that wins the umpire's coin toss chooses whether to be first to bat or in the field.

Softballs look similar to baseballs but are bigger.

THE FIELD AND EQUIPMENT

The official size of a softball field changes for different age groups. For kids under ten, the bases are 55 feet (16.77 meters) apart and the pitcher is 35 feet (10.67 meters) from home plate.

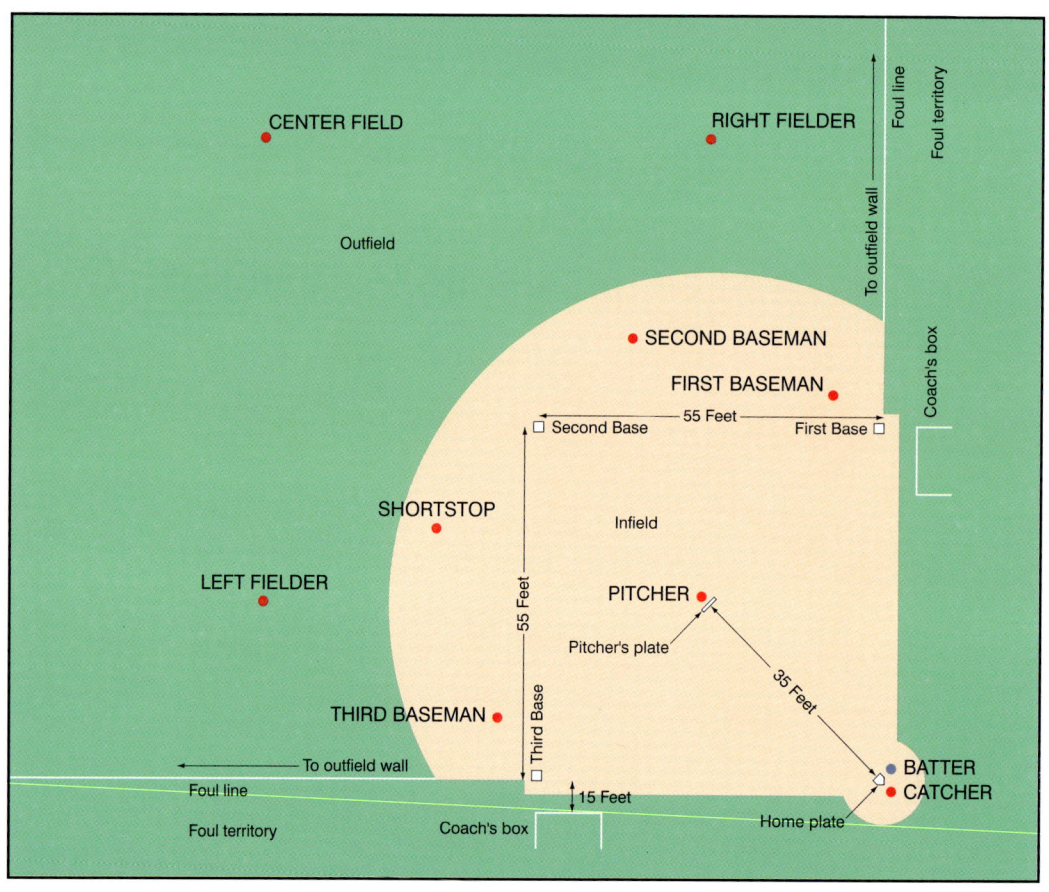

This diagram shows players' positions and the size of a softball field for a kids' game.

A player protects the head by wearing a batting helmet.

The fence, or edge of the outfield, is 150 feet (45.73 meters) from home plate. In adult fast-pitch softball, this distance increases to 265 feet (80.77 meters).

Softballs are larger than baseballs and softball bats are a little bigger around than baseball bats. Gloves, mitts, batting helmets, and catcher's protective equipment are all used in softball.

Players and Substitutes

To play a softball game, each team must have nine players. If a team has less than that, they forfeit the game. In kids' games, there are often ten players, with the extra as a short outfielder.

Substitutes (SUB steh toots) can be used if they are on the batting order. They can be called a **designated** (DEZ ig nay ted) player, pinch hitter, base runner, or defense only (DEFO), depending on which position they play. The umpire must be told when a substitute enters the game. Substitutes are used when a player is tired, like the pitcher, or if using a substitute will help the team score more runs.

All players on a team wait for the pitch.

THE GAME

A softball game is between two teams who each have an equal number of turns to score runs. Runs are scored by a player first hitting the ball with a bat and then running to each base in order before the other team gets the player out.

When a team gets three outs, their turn to score is over. When each team has had a turn at bat, or had their chance to score, it is called an inning.

Most softball games are seven innings long and the team with the most runs after seven innings is the winner. If the teams are tied, extra innings are added until one team wins. For kids there is a limit of one-and-a-half hours for a game.

Before practice, warm-up exercises help prepare the body for playing softball.

The umpire calls strikes, balls, and outs for each team at bat.

PITCHING

Softball pitching must be underhand and every pitch must begin with **presentation** (pree zen TAY shun). This means the pitcher must come to a full stop with shoulders in line with first and third base and with the ball held in both hands in front of his or her body. Both feet must be touching the pitcher's plate.

After presenting the ball, the pitcher starts the pitch.

A long step adds power to a pitch.

The pitch begins when one hand is taken off the ball. Many pitchers have a windup to help them throw the ball. In fast-pitch softball, the ball should **arc** (ARK) no more than six feet (1.83 meters) off the ground and in slow pitch, the ball usually arcs from six to 12 feet (1.83-3.66 meters). A pitcher's goal is to throw, or deliver, the ball to the batter's strike zone, or between the armpits and knees of the batter.

BATTING

Each player takes a turn at bat and has at least three chances to swing at pitches. If the batter swings and misses it is called a strike. A strike is also called if the pitch was in the **strike zone** (STRYK ZONE) and the batter didn't swing. Three strikes equal one out and the batter's turn is over. A pitch that goes outside of the strike zone is called a ball and four balls equal a free walk to first base.

A softball hit into the playing field is a fair ball. Balls hit outside of the white border lines are foul balls. If any fly balls are caught, the batter is out. If the bat just nicks the ball, it is a strike unless there are two strikes already, then it is a foul.

A team is playing offense when at bat and defense when in the field.

The stance is the position the batter takes in the batter's box, ready to swing.

Base Running

After hitting a fair ball, the batter becomes a base runner moving to first base, then second, third, and home.

While the runner is touching a base, he or she cannot be put out. A base runner must touch the base until the pitcher releases the next pitch. Only one runner can touch the same base at a time.

Between bases, the runner can be put out in many ways. A runner between bases is forced out when another runner is safe on the base behind and the ball is thrown to the base ahead of the runner. A base runner can also be **tagged** (TAGD) out.

Rounding the bases means running outside of the baseline and cutting corners off of the bases.

UMPIRES

Umpires are the police of softball. They don't make the rules but they make sure players, coaches, and **spectators** (SPEK tay terz) follow the rules. A game might have both base and plate umpires or just one. Before a game they check the field for anything dangerous. They make sure there is a scorekeeper.

A plate umpire stands behind the catcher and batter.

Umpires watch every play to make sure the rules are followed.

Umpires decide which pitches are balls and which are strikes, which hits are foul or fair, and whether a runner is out or safe. If there is a question about an umpire's call, the coach should ask for a time-out to discuss it. The umpire should be treated with respect and the umpire's decision is final.

DEAD BALL, ALIVE BALL

A ball can be dead (out of play) or alive (in play). A dead ball stops play of the game. When the umpire calls "play," they begin again and continue until the next dead ball.

Some of the situations for a dead ball are when the ball touches a batter, when the umpire calls time-out, when a foul ball is not caught, or when a walk is allowed.

A ball is alive after a fly ball is caught for an out, when a fair ball is hit, or whether a base runner is called out or safe. In fact, the ball remains alive during most of the game.

> The longest fast-pitch softball game was 61 hours, 36 minutes, and 33 seconds with no substitutes on either team. The score was 343-296. It was played in North Carolina in 1984.

If a ball is hit outside of this foul line and is not caught, it is a dead ball.

GLOSSARY

arc (ARK)—curve

designated (DEZ ig nay ted) — a player picked at the beginning of the game to substitute as a batter for the pitcher

innings (IN ingz) — a part of a game where each team has a chance to score before making three outs

presentation (pree zen TAY shun) — to show the ball so everyone can see it

spectators (SPEK tay terz) — the people watching a game

strike zone (STRYK ZONE) — the area over home plate and between the batter's shoulders and knees

substitute (SUB steh toot) — a player who is put in a game in place of another player

tagged (TAGD) — being touched with the ball or with the hand holding the ball

An umpire crouches to see the pitch.

INDEX

ball   5, 11, 12, 13, 14, 17, 20
fast-pitch   5, 13
foul   14, 19, 20
inning   5, 11
out   5, 11, 14, 17, 19, 20
pitcher   5, 6, 8, 12, 13, 17
pitcher's plate   12
run   5, 8, 11
strike   13, 14, 19
umpire   18, 19, 20

FURTHER READING

Find out more about softball with these helpful books and information sites:
Elliott, Jill & Martha Ewing, eds. *Youth Softball: A Complete Handbook.* printed by Brown & Benchmark, 1992
Rookie Coaches Softball Guide/American Sport Education Program. Human Kinetics Publishers, Inc., 1992
Cohen, Neil, ed. *The Everything You Wanted to Know About Sports Encyclopedia.* Bantam Books, 1994
Boehm, David A., editor-in-chief. *Guinness Sports Record Book 1990-91.* Sterling Publishing Co., Inc. 1990

on the internet at
www.softball.com/othrlink.htm (links to organizations, equipment manufacturers, teams, etc)